JERBOA

by Rachel Rose

Minneapolis, Minnesota

Credits
Cover and title page, © Lauren/Adobe Stock; 3 © Lauren Suryanata/Shutterstock; 4–5, © Yerbolat Shadrakhov/Shutterstock; 6L, © Lauren/Adobe Stock; 6R, © Agami Photo Agency/Shutterstock; 7, © Lauren/Adobe Stock; 8–9, © edward-m/Adobe Stock; 10, © Vladone/iStock; 11, © edward-m/Adobe Stock; 13, © Lauren/Adobe Stock; 15, © Nature Picture Library/Alamy Stock Photo; 17, © Yerbolat Shadrakhov/iStock; 18–19, © jindrich_pavelka/Shutterstock; 21, © ChrWeiss/Adobe Stock; 22L, © Tanto Yensen/iStock; 22R, © Far700/iStock; 23, © Jiri Anderle/iStock.

Bearport Publishing Company Product Development Team
President: Jen Jenson; Director of Product Development: Spencer Brinker; Managing Editor: Allison Juda; Associate Editor: Naomi Reich; Associate Editor: Tiana Tran; Art Director: Colin O'Dea; Designer: Kayla Eggert; Product Development Assistant: Owen Hamlin

STATEMENT ON USAGE OF GENERATIVE ARTIFICIAL INTELLIGENCE
Bearport Publishing remains committed to publishing high-quality nonfiction books. Therefore, we restrict the use of generative AI to ensure accuracy of all text and visual components pertaining to a book's subject. See BearportPublishing.com for details.

Library of Congress Cataloging-in-Publication Data is available at www.loc.gov or upon request from the publisher.

ISBN: 979-8-89232-021-4 (hardcover)
ISBN: 979-8-89232-499-1 (paperback)
ISBN: 979-8-89232-146-4 (ebook)

Copyright © 2025 Bearport Publishing Company. All rights reserved. No part of this publication may be reproduced in whole or in part, stored in any retrieval system, or transmitted in any form or by any means, electronic, mechanical, photocopying, recording, or otherwise, without written permission from the publisher. Bearport Publishing is a division of Chrysalis Education Group.

For more information, write to Bearport Publishing, 5357 Penn Avenue South, Minneapolis, MN 55419.

Contents

Awesome Jerboas! 4
Tiny Kangaroos 6
Life in the Desert 8
Hide-and-Seek 10
Speedy Getaway 12
Seasonal Homes 14
Night Creatures 16
Mating Season 18
Motherly Love 20

Information Station 22
Glossary 23
Index 24
Read More 24
Learn More Online 24
About the Author 24

AWESOME Jerboas!

BOING! A jerboa uses its long back legs to spring high up into the air. The **rodent** hops across the desert sand. Tiny and bouncy, jerboas are awesome!

JERBOAS CAN JUMP AS HIGH AS 10 FEET (3 M) INTO THE AIR.

Tiny Kangaroos

There are 33 kinds of jerboas. These small rodents are only between 2 and 6 inches (5 and 15 cm) tall, but their tails are sometimes twice as long as their bodies! Jerboas have long back legs, too. They use their legs and tails together to jump high off the ground.

Different kinds of jerboas have differently sized ears.

WITH BACK LEGS FOUR TIMES LONGER THAN THEIR FRONT LEGS, JERBOAS LOOK LIKE MINI KANGAROOS.

7

Life in the Desert

Jerboas live in the deserts of eastern Europe, northern Africa, and Asia. These tiny animals have many **adaptations** that help them live in their dry and sandy **habitats**. During hot summers, they flap their big ears to keep themselves cool. **WHOOSH!** They also have hairs inside their ears to keep sand from getting in.

Hide-and-Seek

Soft fur the same color as their sandy surroundings helps jerboas blend in, keeping them hidden from **predators**. Foxes, big cats, owls, and snakes all hunt jerboas. Luckily, their tiny size along with their coloring makes jerboas hard to find in the desert.

IN THE PAST, HUMANS ALSO HUNTED JERBOAS FOR FOOD.

Speedy Getaway

When an unlucky jerboa is spotted by a predator, it escapes by hopping away. Not only can jerboas jump very high, but they are also super fast. They can get away at speeds as fast as 15 miles per hour (24 kph). **ZOOM!** To confuse their predators, jerboas move in zigzags.

JERBOAS USE THEIR EXCELLENT HEARING TO LISTEN FOR NEARBY PREDATORS.

Seasonal Homes

These desert animals make their homes, called **burrows**, in the sand. Jerboas dig different burrows for different purposes. To keep themselves safe from danger, jerboas build **temporary** burrows where they can run to and hide in. During hot summers, they build bigger burrows that they use for longer stretches of time. Jerboas plug them up with soil during the day to keep the heat out.

SOME JERBOAS ALSO BUILD WINTER BURROWS WHERE THEY CAN STAY WARM AS THEY **HIBERNATE**.

A jerboa digging a burrow

Night Creatures

When things cool down at night, jerboas come out of their burrows to look for food. These **nocturnal** animals eat mostly plants and small insects, such as beetles. *CRUNCH!* Jerboas feed on seeds, too. These rodents use their big eyes and long whiskers to find their way in the dark.

> JERBOAS DON'T DRINK. THEY GET ALL THE WATER THEY NEED FROM THE PLANTS THEY EAT!

Mating Season

Jerboas usually live alone. They look for others only when it's time to **mate**. After the cold winter months come to an end, **male** jerboas seek out partners. Up to 35 days later, **female** jerboas have babies. They can give birth to as many as six babies at a time, but more often jerboas have only three.

MALE JERBOAS OFTEN MATE WITH MANY FEMALES, WHILE FEMALES MATE WITH JUST ONE MALE.

Motherly Love

Jerboa babies, called pups, are teeny-tiny when they are born. They have no fur, and their back legs are not ready to jump yet. Their mother looks after them until the babies can take care of themselves. When they are about 11 weeks old, the young jerboas are grown enough to hop away and live on their own.

JERBOAS CAN LIVE UP TO SIX YEARS IN THE WILD.

Jerboa pups

Information Station

JERBOAS ARE AWESOME!
LET'S LEARN EVEN MORE ABOUT THEM.

Kind of animal: Jerboas are mammals. Most mammals have fur, give birth to live young, and drink milk from their mothers as babies.

More jerboas: Of the 33 kinds of jerboas, long-eared jerboas have the biggest ears. The big ears are two-thirds the size of their bodies.

Size: The smallest jerboas grow to only about 2 in. (5 cm) tall. That's the same height as an AA battery!

JERBOAS AROUND THE WORLD

Arctic Ocean
EUROPE
ASIA
NORTH AMERICA
Pacific Ocean
Atlantic Ocean
AFRICA
Pacific Ocean
SOUTH AMERICA
Indian Ocean
AUSTRALIA
Southern Ocean
ANTARCTICA

■ WHERE JERBOAS LIVE

Glossary

adaptations special skills or parts of the body that help an animal survive

burrows holes or tunnels dug by an animal to live in

female a jerboa that can give birth to young

habitats places in nature where animals live

hibernate to spend the winter in a deep sleep

male a jerboa that cannot give birth to young

mate to come together in order to have young

nocturnal active only at night

predators animals that hunt and kill other animals for food

rodent a small mammal that has sharp front teeth

temporary lasting for only a short time

Index

burrows 14–16
desert 4, 8, 10, 14
female 18–19
food 11, 16
habitats 8
hibernate 14
male 18–19
mate 18–19
predators 10, 12, 14
pups 20–21
rodents 4, 6, 16
summer 8, 14
winter 14, 18

Read More

McHale, Brenda. *Animals in the Sand (Animal Fact Files).* Minneapolis: Bearport Publishing Company, 2023.

Sabelko, Rebecca. *Desert Animals (What Animal Am I?).* Minneapolis: Bellwether Media, Inc., 2023.

Learn More Online

1. Go to **www.factsurfer.com** or scan the QR code below.
2. Enter "**Jerboa**" into the search box.
3. Click on the cover of this book to see a list of websites.

About the Author

Rachel Rose writes books for kids and teaches yoga. Her favorite animal for all time is her dog, Sandy.